CONTENTS

Introduction

CARS

The fastest cars have room for
a driver, passenger and not
much else! These machines are
certainly not a sensible family

car – they are built for speed. They are low to the ground
with an aerodynamic body and a powerful engine. Sports
cars are admired all over the world. They are not just
beautiful pieces of engineering, they are works of art.

PLANES

The first plane flew in 1903.
Aviation technology developed
quickly, and now millions of passengers travel by plane
each year. Planes are flying faster and further than ever
before. Today, some of the most exciting new aircraft are
being developed by the military.

SUPERBIKES

Motorbikes have always symbolised the freedom of the road and an escape from everyday life. The machines in this book would make that escape easier than ever before. They are some of the fastest bikes in production. These are not just motorbikes, they are superbikes.

BOATS

All boats float on water, have a means of power and a way for the crew to control speed and direction. But the variation in boat design is immense. Some are built for short journeys in safe waters, others brave the worst weather on the open sea. The boats in this book celebrate the amazing diversity of travel by water.

ASTON MARTIN V12 VANQUISH

The British firm Aston Martin made their first sports car back in 1914. Nearly ninety years later the **V12** Vanquish went on sale. With a powerful **engine** and a **body** made out of the lightweight metal **aluminium**, the four-seater Vanquish is one of the fastest cars in the world.

DID YOU KNOW?

In the film "Die Another Day", the super spy James Bond drives a V12 Vanquish.

The car has **tyre** pressure sensors, rain sensors and even sensors that switch the headlights on when it gets too dark.

The V12 has **Formula One**-style **gearchange paddles** behind the steering wheel. You click right to change up a **gear**, and left to change down.

STATS AND FACTS

LAUNCHED: *2001*

ORIGIN: *UK*

ENGINE: *5,935 cc V12, front-mounted*

MAX POWER: *460 bhp at 6,800 rpm*

MAX TORQUE: *400 lb per ft at 5,500 rpm*

MAX SPEED: *190 mph*

ACCELERATION: *0-60 mph: 4.5 seconds*

WEIGHT: *1.83 tonnes*

COST: *£158,000*

The body panels are shaped by hand to make sure the edges are perfect.

BMW Z8

The Z8 is a modern sports car with old fashioned looks. This **roadster** is based on the beautiful BMW 507 built in the 1950s. Thanks to the enormous power from its **V8 engine**, the Z8 is more than just beautiful. Without the electronic speed reducer the top speed would be 180 mph.

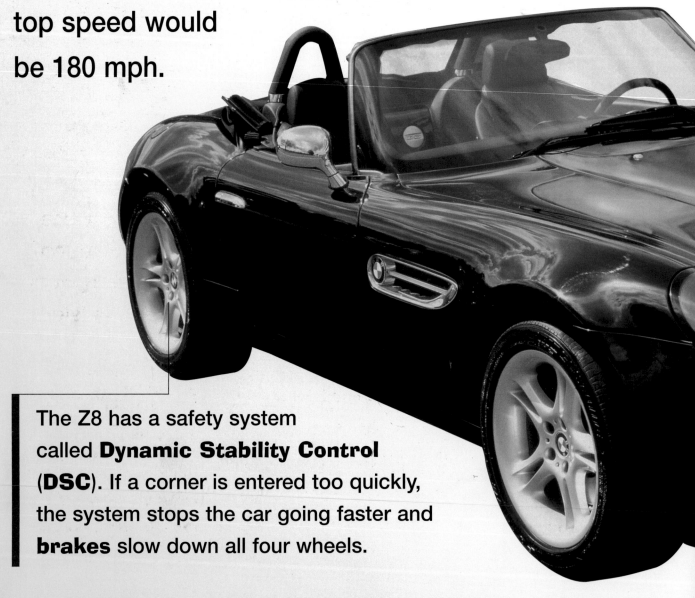

The Z8 has a safety system called **Dynamic Stability Control** (**DSC**). If a corner is entered too quickly, the system stops the car going faster and **brakes** slow down all four wheels.

The dials are unusually placed in the centre of the **dashboard**. This gives the driver a clear view of the road.

STATS AND FACTS

LAUNCHED: *2000*

ORIGIN: *Germany*

ENGINE: *4,941 cc 32-valve V8, front-mounted*

MAX POWER: *400 bhp at 6,600 rpm*

MAX TORQUE: *369 lb per ft at 3,800 rpm*

MAX SPEED: *155 mph (limited)*

ACCELERATION: *0-60 mph: 4.8 seconds*

WEIGHT: *1.58 tonnes*

COST: *£85,000*

Z8 customers can choose between a hard top or a soft top for their roadster.

DID YOU KNOW?

The Z8's satellite navigation system is hidden behind a flap in the dashboard.

BUGATTI EB 110

The Italian firm Bugatti was the biggest car maker in the world before it went bankrupt in the 1950s. Its famous name was brought back to life in 1987 and plans were made for a new car. Sadly Bugatti made just 356 EB 110's before they closed again in 1996.

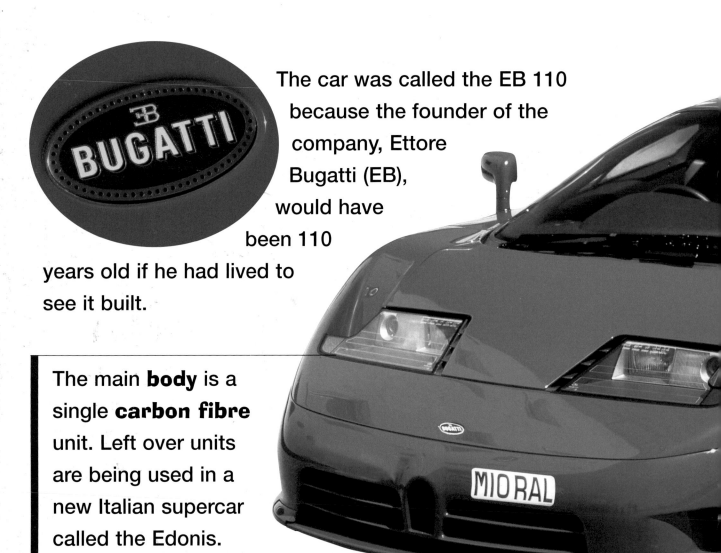

The car was called the EB 110 because the founder of the company, Ettore Bugatti (EB), would have been 110 years old if he had lived to see it built.

The main **body** is a single **carbon fibre** unit. Left over units are being used in a new Italian supercar called the Edonis.

On the outside, the EB 110 looks like a car of the future. But inside it has a wooden **dashboard**, as you might find in an old sports car.

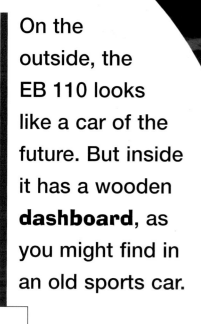

STATS AND FACTS

LAUNCHED: *1991*

ORIGIN: *Built in France*

ENGINE: *3,500 cc 60-valve V12, mid-mounted*

MAX POWER: *553 bhp at 8,000 rpm*

MAX TORQUE: *451 lb per ft at 3,250 rpm*

MAX SPEED: *209 mph*

ACCELERATION: *0-60 mph: 3.4 seconds*

WEIGHT: *1.56 tonnes*

COST: *£343,100*

DID YOU KNOW?

Ettore Bugatti was Italian but he spent most of his life in France and built his factory there.

CHEVROLET CORVETTE Z06

The American car company Chevrolet built their first Corvette in 1953. It soon became the world's most popular sports car. By 2002, millions of Corvettes had been sold all over the world. The reason for the car's success is simple. The Corvette is very fast but comes at a reasonable price.

DID YOU KNOW?

Over 200 of the earliest Corvettes have survived. They are now highly collectable.

In 1999 Chevrolet gave the Corvette a fighter plane-style display. Speed, **revolutions-per-minute (rpm)** and fuel levels are projected onto the windscreen.

STATS AND FACTS

LAUNCHED: *1997*

ORIGIN: *USA*

ENGINE: *5,666 cc V8, front-mounted*

MAX POWER: *385 bhp at 6,000 rpm*

MAX TORQUE: *385 lb per ft at 4,800 rpm*

MAX SPEED: *175 mph*

ACCELERATION: *0-60 mph: 4 seconds*

WEIGHT: *1.41 tonnes*

COST: *£37,999*

This beautiful Corvette was built in 1960. Its powerful **V8 engine** gave a top speed of 130 mph. The average top speed of cars at that time was just 50 mph.

Today the Corvette comes in three **body** styles. **Coupé** (hard top) for winter driving, **Targa** (with solid lift-out roof panel) and **Convertible** (soft top) for the summer.

FERRARI F50

Ferrari is one of the most famous makers of sports cars in the world. The F50 is one of the most exclusive models ever built. Just 349 cars were built to celebrate the Italian legend's 50th anniversary. This incredible car is powered by a slightly less powerful version of a 1990 **Formula One** engine.

The F50's **body**, doors and seats are made from lightweight **carbon fibre**.

STATS AND FACTS

LAUNCHED: *1996*

ORIGIN: *Italy*

ENGINE: *4,699 cc 60-valve V12, mid-mounted*

MAX POWER: *520 bhp at 8,500 rpm*

MAX TORQUE: *347 lb per ft at 6,500 rpm*

MAX SPEED: *202 mph*

ACCELERATION: *0-60 mph: 3.7 seconds*

WEIGHT: *1.23 tonnes*

COST: *£342,700*

Underneath the car the body is completely flat. The four **exhausts** stick out through holes cut into the rear, just like a racing car.

The engine is in the middle of the F50. It powers the Ferrari to 60 mph in under 4 seconds. The car goes from 0-100 mph in just 8 seconds and 0-150 mph in 18 seconds.

DID YOU KNOW?

The F50 is a very expensive car. But you still have to wind the windows up and down by hand!

JAGUAR XJ220S

In the late 1980s, the British car maker Jaguar decided to build a **supercar**. They called it the XJ220. In 1992 the first models were delivered to customers, costing £415,000 each. Two years later, Jaguar produced an even faster, lighter and cheaper version of the car. It was called the XJ220S.

DID YOU KNOW?

In 1994 racing driver Martin Brundle reached 217 mph in an XJ220S. At the time this was the fastest speed ever recorded by a road car.

The back of the car has an enormous wing. It stretches right across the body of one of the widest sports cars ever made.

STATS AND FACTS

LAUNCHED: *1994*

ORIGIN: *UK*

ENGINE: *3,498 cc twin-turbo V6, mid-mounted*

MAX POWER: *680 bhp at 7,200 rpm*

MAX TORQUE: *527 lb per ft at 5,000 rpm*

MAX SPEED: *217 mph*

ACCELERATION: *0-60 mph: 3.3 seconds*

WEIGHT: *1.08 tonnes*

COST: *£293,750*

The XJ220S was built by TWR (Tom Walkinshaw Racing). They based their design on the XJ220C cars that took part in the Le Mans race in France in 1993.

The XJ220's **aluminium** body was replaced with **carbon fibre** to make the XJ220S even lighter. The power was also increased from 542 **bhp** to 680 bhp.

LAMBORGHINI MURCIÉLAGO

Ferrucio Lamborghini was a millionaire tractor maker from northern Italy. Unhappy with the Ferrari he owned he decided he could build a better car himself. In 1966 Lamborghini made the first real **supercar**, the Miura. In 2001, the company started selling their tenth model, the Murciélago.

The roof and the doors of the Murciélago are made of steel. The rest of the car is made from **carbon fibre**.

DID YOU KNOW?

The Lamborghini badge features a charging bull, a symbol of both beauty and violence.

To reverse the Murciélago, most drivers flip open a door, and sit on the edge of the car. They can then look over their shoulder to see where they are going!

STATS AND FACTS

LAUNCHED: *2001*

ORIGIN: *Italy*

ENGINE: *6,192 cc V12, mid-mounted*

MAX POWER: *571 bhp at 7,500 rpm*

MAX TORQUE: *479 lb per ft at 5,400 rpm*

MAX SPEED: *205 mph*

ACCELERATION: *0-60 mph: 4 seconds*

WEIGHT: *1.65 tonnes*

COST: *£163,000*

The Murciélago is easier to drive than previous Lamborghinis. It has **four-wheel drive** and a safety system that slows the car down if it starts to lose its grip on the road.

McLAREN F1

McLaren are famous makers of **Formula One** cars. In 1993 the firm decided to make the ultimate **supercar**. The result was the F1. It was the first car costing one million dollars, and the fastest road car ever.

DID YOU KNOW?

An annual service for the McLaren F1 costs an amazing £25,000!

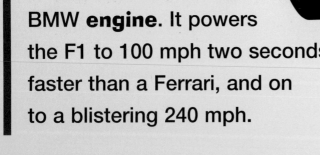

The back of the car is taken up by the huge BMW **engine**. It powers the F1 to 100 mph two seconds faster than a Ferrari, and on to a blistering 240 mph.

STATS AND FACTS

LAUNCHED: *1993*

ORIGIN: *UK*

ENGINE: *6,064 cc 48-valve V12, mid-mounted*

MAX POWER: *627 bhp at 7,400 rpm*

MAX TORQUE: *479 lb per ft at 7,000 rpm*

MAX SPEED: *240.1 mph*

ACCELERATION:
0-60 mph: 3.2 seconds
0-100 mph: 6.3 seconds

WEIGHT: *1.14 tonnes*

COST: *£634,500*

The F1's central driving position is unusual for a supercar. The two rear seats are also unusual for a sports car.

A total of 100 F1 road cars were built before McLaren stopped making them in 1998. Each one took nearly two months to build!

PAGANI ZONDA C12 S

This car was designed by an Argentinian called Horacio Pagani. It is named after a wind that blows from the Andes mountains in Argentina. The Pagani Zonda is the newest and most exclusive **supercar**. There were only 30 built in the first year.

DID YOU KNOW?

When you buy a Zonda, you get a pair of driving shoes made for you by the Pope's shoe maker.

The Zonda has no boot at all! The only luggage space is behind the seats.

This C12 S model has a massive 7.3 litre **V12 engine**. It is made by AMG, who make racing car engines for Mercedes-Benz.

STATS AND FACTS

LAUNCHED: *2001*

ORIGIN: *Italy*

ENGINE: *7,010 cc V12, mid-mounted*

MAX POWER: *562 bhp at 5,500 rpm*

MAX TORQUE: *553 lb per ft at 4,100 rpm*

MAX SPEED: *220 mph*

ACCELERATION: *0-60 mph: 3.7 seconds*

WEIGHT: *1.25 tonnes*

COST: *£298,000*

The Zonda looks like a fighter plane. It has a glass-roofed cabin, twin **spoilers** and a rocket-style **exhaust**. The inside is made of **aluminium**, suede, leather and **carbon fibre**.

PORSCHE 911 GT2

On the outside the GT2 looks like an ordinary Porsche 911 Turbo. But inside all of the luxuries have been removed to make the car drive like a racing car. There is harder **suspension**, a **rollcage**, special **brakes** and a lot of extra power! The GT2 costs £30,000 more than the Turbo, but it is the fastest 911 ever.

DID YOU KNOW?

The GT2 is the fastest road car in Porsche's history, capable of 197 mph.

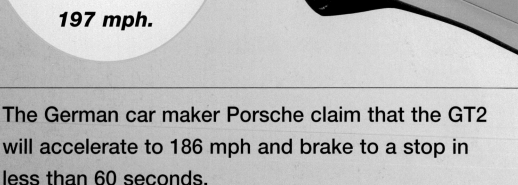

The German car maker Porsche claim that the GT2 will accelerate to 186 mph and brake to a stop in less than 60 seconds.

STATS AND FACTS

The rear wing and side panels have vents to cool the huge **engine**. There are also vents in the **nose** and slats in the bonnet. They direct air to cool the **radiator** and brakes.

LAUNCHED: *2001*

ORIGIN: *Germany*

ENGINE: *3,600 cc 24-valve turbo Flat 6, rear-mounted*

MAX POWER: *455 bhp at 5,700 rpm*

MAX TORQUE: *459 lb per ft at 3,500 rpm*

MAX SPEED: *197 mph*

ACCELERATION: *0-62 mph: 4.1 seconds*

WEIGHT: *1.44 tonnes*

COST: *£109,800*

The GT2 is 10 percent more powerful and 7 percent lighter than the 911 Turbo.

TVR TUSCAN

TVR are based in England. They have been making affordable sports cars for over forty years. In 2000 the firm started selling the Tuscan. They made the car as light as possible and gave it a huge **engine**. The result is an amazingly fast car that costs far less than its rivals.

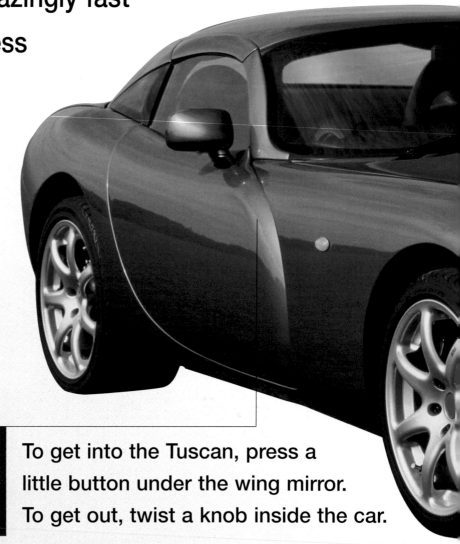

To get into the Tuscan, press a little button under the wing mirror. To get out, twist a knob inside the car.

STATS AND FACTS

LAUNCHED: *2000*

ORIGIN: *UK*

ENGINE: *3,605 cc 24 valve Inline 6, front-mounted*

MAX POWER: *350 bhp at 7,200 rpm*

MAX TORQUE: *290 lb per ft at 5,500 rpm*

MAX SPEED: *180 mph*

ACCELERATION: *0-60 mph: 4.4 seconds*

WEIGHT: *1.1 tonnes*

COST: *£39,850*

The roof and the rear window can be taken off and stored in the Tuscan's large boot. There is even enough space left over for a couple of suitcases!

GDB 341

The Tuscan's engine uses most of the space under the bonnet. It powers the car to 180 mph.

AIRBUS A380

Ever since the first plane took to the skies, aircraft have got bigger and bigger. In 1970 the American firm Boeing produced the enormous 747. In 2006, a new giant started flying, the enormous Airbus A380. It was built by the European company, Airbus.

The body of the A380 is deeper and wider than a 747. There are two **engines** on each **wing**.

Airbus's A380 monster is a double decker plane, carrying passengers on two spacious decks.

STATS AND FACTS

LAUNCHED: *2006*

ORIGIN: *Europe*

MODELS: *Five passenger versions, and the A380-800F for cargo*

ENGINES: *Four Rolls-Royce Trent 900 engines providing 36,280 kg thrust or four Engine Alliance GP7200 turbofans, rated at 37,003 kg thrust*

WINGSPAN: *79.8 metres*

LENGTH: *73 metres*

CREW: *Two*

SEATING: *Up to 8000*

MAX SPEED: *588 mph*

MAX WEIGHT: *590 tonnes*

RANGE: *9,378 miles*

LOAD: *Up to 800 passengers or 150 tonnes of cargo*

COST: *£154 million*

The standard A380 has room for 555 passengers, travelling in economy, business and first classes. But seating is flexible, and some airlines might choose all-economy seating, and carry up to 800 people.

SR-71 BLACKBIRD

In 1960 the USSR shot down a US spy plane. After this disaster the American military were ordered to make a craft that would never be shot down again. The result was the amazing SR-71, packed with cameras and **sensors**. In 20 years of dangerous missions, no Blackbird was ever lost in combat.

DID YOU KNOW?

The Blackbird once flew from New York–London in 1 hour 55 minutes.

WARNING
Restricted Area

STATS AND FACTS

LAUNCHED: *1962*

ORIGIN: *USA*

MODELS: *SR-71A, SR-71B and SR-71C*

ENGINES: *Two Pratt & Whitney J58-P-10s with afterburners, providing 14,724 kg thrust each*

WINGSPAN: *16.94 metres*

LENGTH: *31.65 metres*

CREW: *Two*

MAX SPEED: *2,250 mph (Mach 3.4)*

MAX WEIGHT: *78 tonnes*

RANGE: *3,000 miles*

LOAD: *Sensors and powerful cameras*

COST: *£33 million (in 1962)*

The Blackbird was made in top secrecy. President Johnson refused to admit that it even existed until 1964.

Each **engine** has enough **thrust** to power an ocean liner. The large spikes catch air to keep the plane balanced in flight.

The SR-71's are made of a special material called **titanium alloy**. It protects the planes from the extreme heat produced flying at such high speeds.

B-2 SPIRIT

Stealth technology has developed very quickly. By 1978 it was possible to design an aircraft that was almost invisible to **radar**. One of the most striking of these planes was the B-2. The first model flew in July 1989, and looked like it came from another planet.

DID YOU KNOW?

The B-2's skin is jet black and smooth. All the joints are carefully concealed.

The B-2 is really just a giant **wing** with sharp edges. The strange bulges hide the plane's **engines**, **cockpit** and bombs.

STATS AND FACTS

LAUNCHED: *1989*

ORIGIN: *USA*

MODELS: *The US Air Force has 20 planes, all slightly different*

ENGINES: *Four General Electric F118-GE-110 turbofans each rated at 8,618 kg thrust*

WINGSPAN: *52.43 metres*

LENGTH: *21.03 metres*

CREW: *Two*

MAX SPEED: *630 mph*

MAX WEIGHT: *181.4 tonnes*

RANGE: *7,644 miles*

LOAD: *Up to 22.6 tonnes of many types of nuclear or conventional bombs, missiles or mines*

COST: *£1.6 billion*

The plane has just two crew on board. The rest of the cockpit is taken up by computer-controlled flight equipment.

The B-2 is stuffed full of computers and heat and noise reducing technology. It is the world's most expensive aircraft. In 1998 each plane cost an amazing £1.6 billion!

B-52 STRATOFORTRESS

After World War 2,
the US Air Force decided
to create huge aircraft
that would put people
off starting wars.
They were called the
B-52's, and were
monster eight-**engined** jet bombers. In 1952 the
first of these giants took to the skies.

DID YOU KNOW?

There are six ejection seats on a B-52 in case of emergency.

The B-52 has **sensors**
that let the plane fly
very close to the ground
during combat missions.

This B-52D has eight powerful engines. Despite their size, they burn less fuel than those found on earlier models.

STATS AND FACTS

LAUNCHED: *1952*

ORIGIN: *USA*

MODELS: *XB-52, YB-52 (1952), B-52A to B-52H (1954-65)*

ENGINES: *Eight 7,711 kg thrust Pratt & Whitney TF33 turbofan engines*

WINGSPAN: *56.39 metres*

LENGTH: *49.05 metres*

CREW: *Six*

MAX SPEED: *595 mph*

MAX WEIGHT: *256.7 tonnes*

RANGE: *12,566 miles*

LOAD: *Nuclear or high-explosive bombs, cruise missiles and a variety of guns*

COST: *£6 million (in 1952)*

This B-52 is being refuelled in flight. **Air refuelling** allows B-52s to fly almost anywhere in the world.

EUROFIGHTER TYPHOON

European countries get together to develop new warplanes. For each partner this is cheaper than developing an aircraft by themselves. The latest example is the Typhoon, developed by Britain, Germany, Italy and Spain.

DID YOU KNOW?

The idea for a Eurofighter dates back to 1979. However, it was over 20 years before the first Typhoon was built.

Only 15% of the outside of the Eurofighter's body is made of metal. The rest is mainly lightweight **carbon fibre** that lets it cruise at great speeds without overheating.

STATS AND FACTS

LAUNCHED: *2002*

ORIGIN: *Europe*

MODELS: *Single seat and two seat versions*

ENGINES: *Two Eurojet EJ200 reheated turbofans each providing 9,072 kg thrust*

WINGSPAN: *10.95 metres*

LENGTH: *15.96 metres*

CREW: *One or two*

MAX SPEED: *1,323 mph (Mach 2)*

MAX WEIGHT: *21 tonnes*

RANGE: *1,800 miles*

LOAD: *One 27-mm gun (not used by UK) and up to 8 tonnes of missiles or bombs on 13 attachments*

COST: *£20 million*

The Typhoon has two **engines**. It also has a large triangular **wing** and small powered **foreplanes** on each side of the nose. The Typhoon comes in one or two seat versions.

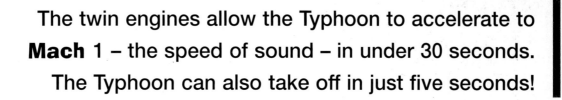

The twin engines allow the Typhoon to accelerate to **Mach** 1 – the speed of sound – in under 30 seconds. The Typhoon can also take off in just five seconds!

F-117A NIGHTHAWK

First flown in 1981, the F-117A is perhaps the weirdest aircraft ever made. Its shape is designed to break up enemy **radar** signals. Because it can be **air refuelled**, the F-117A can travel almost anywhere in the world. This amazing plane is made by the US firm Lockheed.

DID YOU KNOW?

The only non-black parts of the F-117A are the windows.

The F-117A is made up of hundreds of flat surfaces. These deflect enemy **radar** and make the plane almost invisible.

STATS AND FACTS

The F-117A is not really a fighter plane but a bomber. It carries its weapons inside, behind doors with zigzag edges. They open and shut very quickly to release bombs.

LAUNCHED: *1981*

ORIGIN: *USA*

MODELS: *Five prototypes and 59 production aircraft*

ENGINES: *Two General Electric F404-F1D2 special turbofans, each giving 4,899 kg thrust*

WINGSPAN: *13.2 metres*

LENGTH: *20.08 metres*

CREW: *One*

MAX SPEED: *700 mph (Mach 1)*

MAX WEIGHT: *23.8 tonnes*

RANGE: *Without air refuelling about 1,500 miles*

LOAD: *Usually two 907 kg laser-guided bombs*

COST: *£75 million*

There are three F-117A's on display in the USA. One is on view to the public at the United States Air Force Museum. You can walk right up to this incredible plane.

HARRIER

By the end of the 1950s air forces started asking for planes that could operate from backyards, forest clearings or even small ships. To meet this need, Hawker Aircraft in England launched one of the first **VTOL** (vertical takeoff and landing) aircraft in 1969. This plane was called the Harrier.

DID YOU KNOW?

The US Marine Corps use the Harrier to provide air power for a force invading an enemy shore.

This single-seat Sea Harrier operates from ships.
There are also two-seater versions and trainer versions.

Harriers have a special system called **VIFF**. It lets them perform impossible manoeuvres to confuse enemy fighter pilots.

STATS AND FACTS

LAUNCHED: *1969*

ORIGIN: *Britain*

MODELS: *Seven versions*

ENGINES: *One Rolls-Royce Pegasus vectored thrust turbofan giving 8,618 kg thrust*

WINGSPAN: *13.2 metres*

LENGTH: *14.1 metres*

CREW: *One to two*

MAX SPEED: *700 mph (Mach 1)*

MAX WEIGHT: *14 tonnes*

RANGE: *Without air refuelling about 1,700 miles*

LOAD: *Missiles, rockets and bombs*

COST: *£40 million*

The **engine** has two nozzles on each side. They blast to the rear for high speed; downwards for takeoff or landing; or forwards to slow down.

JOINT STRIKE FIGHTER

In 1995 the USAF and US Navy launched a programme for a JSF (Joint Strike Fighter). Their aim was to produce the next generation of advanced planes for airfields and aircraft carriers.

DID YOU KNOW?

While the original partners expect to buy 3,002 F-35s, sales to other countries are likely to double this total.

All JSF models carry weapons in two bays on each side of the **fuselage**.

The rear **exhaust** produces **thrust** to lift the aircraft. The X-35B is given extra lift by a fan that takes power from the engine.

STATS AND FACTS

LAUNCHED: *1995*

ORIGIN: *USA*

MODELS: *X-35A, X-35B and X-35C, described below*

ENGINES: *One Pratt & Whitney F135 turbofan delivering 18,144 kg thrust, with one Rolls-Royce Allison engine-driven lift fan on the X-35B*

WINGSPAN: *Up to 13.26 metres*

LENGTH: *15.39 metres*

CREW: *One*

MAX SPEED: *1,058 mph (Mach 1.6)*

MAX WEIGHT: *27.2 tonnes*

RANGE: *About 1,380 miles*

LOAD: *Enormous variety of guns, missiles and bombs up to 7.7 tonnes*

COST: *£66 million*

There are three versions of the JSF. The X-35A is the basic version. The X-35B comes with a more powerful **engine**. The X-35C (*left*) has a bigger **wing**, which can fold.

SPACE SHUTTLE

The first space flights relied on rockets, giant tubes which stood upright and were fired into orbit. Then in April 1981 the Shuttle was launched. It was the first spacecraft that could be brought back to Earth.

Enterprise

United States

NASA

DID YOU KNOW?

The Shuttle's boosters fall off into the sea. They are recovered and used again.

At the front is an area for up to ten crew, including two **pilots**. In the middle is a large **bay** for **satellites**. At the back are three big rocket **engines**.

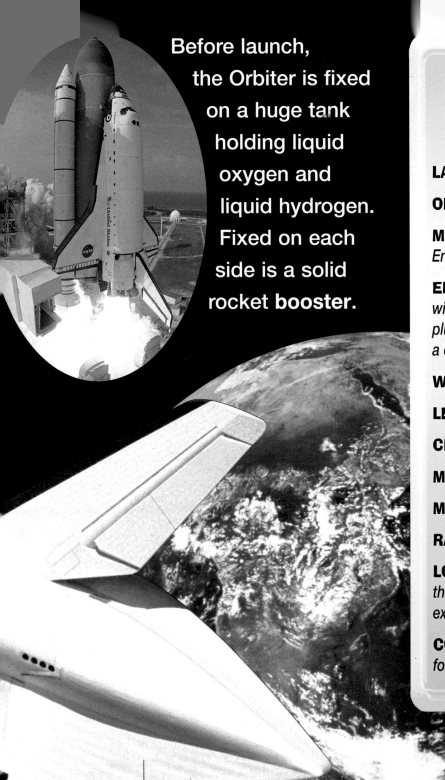

Before launch, the Orbiter is fixed on a huge tank holding liquid oxygen and liquid hydrogen. Fixed on each side is a solid rocket **booster**.

STATS AND FACTS

LAUNCHED: *1981*

ORIGIN: *USA*

MODELS: *Discovery, Atlantis, Endeavour and Colombia*

ENGINES: *Three orbiter engines with combined thrust of 540,000 kg, plus two solid–rocket boosters with a combined thrust of 2,610,000 kg*

WINGSPAN: *23.79 metres*

LENGTH: *56.14 metres*

CREW: *Up to ten*

MAX SPEED: *17,440 mph*

MAX WEIGHT: *2.041 tonnes*

RANGE: *116-403 miles*

LOAD: *Satellites, components for the joint space station and space experiments*

COST: *£1.25 billion plus £294 million for each launch*

After the mission the Shuttle returns to Earth. It is protected by heat-resistant tiles. The Shuttle glides without engine power onto a runway, and is slowed down by a big **parachute**.

VOYAGER

On 23rd December 1986 a strange looking airplane landed at Edwards Air Force Base, California. It had taken off from the same runway nine days previously and flown round the world non-stop. This had never been done before.

DID YOU KNOW?

During its epic journey, Voyager covered 24,986 miles non-stop.

The Voyager was flown by two people. They laid down in a tiny space with a **propeller** at each end. The body was fixed on the centre of a fantastic **wing**.

Voyager was made from **carbon fibre** and **glass fibre**. At rest, its wings scraped on the ground, but in flight they curved upwards like the wings of a bird.

STATS AND FACTS

LAUNCHED: *1985*

ORIGIN: *USA*

MODELS: *One*

ENGINES: *Two Teledyne Continental engines (front 130 bhp, rear 110 bhp)*

WINGSPAN: *33.77 metres*

LENGTH: *8.9 metres*

CREW: *Two*

MAXIMUM SPEED: *122 mph*

MAXIMUM WEIGHT: *4.4 tonnes*

RANGE: *27,455 miles*

LOAD: *Two crew*

COST: *£1 million*

The Voyager was one of many weird looking airplanes created by Bert Rutan. It was flown around the world by his brother Dick, with co-pilot Jeana Yeager.

X-43A

NASA (National Air and Space Administration) is best known for making space rockets. It also carries out important research into aircraft. The X-43A is one of the latest research planes. It is used to find out the best shape to fly at very high speeds in the upper part of the atmosphere.

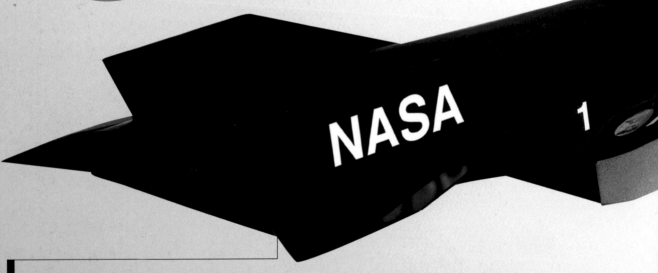

NASA   1

The X-43A has a wide bottom, flat top and two fins. It is powered by a powerful **Scramjet** engine, which burns hydrogen-based fuel.

When launched, the X-43 will travel at between **Mach** 7 and Mach 10, or 4,620–6,600 mph. This means it could travel from London to New York in just 40 minutes, a journey that usually takes seven hours!

STATS AND FACTS

LAUNCHED: *2001 (test version)*

ORIGIN: *USA*

MODELS: *Three test models, each slightly different*

ENGINE: *GASL hydrogen-fuelled scramjet engine*

WINGSPAN: *1.5 metres*

LENGTH: *3.66 metres*

CREW: *Unmanned at present*

MAX SPEED: *6,600 mph (Mach 10)*

MAX WEIGHT: *1.3 tonnes*

RANGE: *Unknown*

COST: *£250 million*

The X-43A's first flight took place on 2 June 2001. It was dropped from a B-52 over the Pacific Ocean. However, the plane broke up in the sky, and NASA is still trying to work out what went wrong.

APRILIA RSV MILLE R

The Italian company Aprilia first became known as a maker of bicycles. Then, in 1968, they began producing motorcycles and mopeds. In 2002, Aprilia launched the Mille R. This beautiful machine is big, fast and very comfortable to ride. The 'R' stands for racing, as this bike is the fastest machine Aprilia have ever made.

DID YOU KNOW?

'Mille' is the Italian word for 'one thousand'. The RSV is called a 'Mille' because the engine is almost 1000 cc.

Up until the end of 2001, all Mille R's were single seat bikes. Then in 2002 Aprilia made a two seater version.

One of the most eye-catching features of the Aprilia is its triple **headlight**.

STATS AND FACTS

LAUNCHED: *2002*

ORIGIN: *Italy*

ENGINE: *997.6 cc*

CYLINDERS: *2*

MAX POWER: *128 bhp at 9,500 rpm*

MAX TORQUE: *101 NM at 7,400 rpm*

GEARS: *6*

DRY WEIGHT: *168 kg*

MAX SPEED: *168 mph*

FUEL TANK CAPACITY: *18 litres*

COLOURS: *Aprilia Black or Flashy Yellow*

COST: *£9,999*

The new Mille has special **radial brakes** at the front. These are much stronger than normal brakes, so the bike can stop very quickly if it needs to.

BENELLI TORNADO

This Italian company was founded in 1911 by a widow called Teresa Benelli. She started the business to provide jobs for her six sons. The Benelli Mechanical Workshop started off making spare parts for cars and motorcycles. Then in 1921 the company made their first motorcycle. In 2002 Benelli started selling the Tornado, a 162 mph **superbike**.

The Tornado's **engine** is also used as part of the bike's **frame**. This makes the bike stronger.

DID YOU KNOW?

The Benelli is built in Italy. But it was designed by an Englishman, and uses suspension made in Sweden.

STATS AND FACTS

LAUNCHED: *2002*

ORIGIN: *Italy*

ENGINE: *898 cc*

CYLINDERS: *3*

MAX POWER: *147 bhp at 11,500 rpm*

MAX TORQUE: *100 NM at 8,500 rpm*

GEARS: *6*

DRY WEIGHT: *185 kg*

MAX SPEED: *162 mph (est)*

FUEL TANK CAPACITY: *18 litres*

COLOURS: *Green/Silver*

COST: *£22,000*

The Tornado's **radiator** is under the seat. Two big **fans** suck in air to cool the radiator.

A more powerful, racing version of the Tornado has competed at the World Superbike Championships. It was designed by Italian Riccardo Rosa, who has worked with the Italian car company Ferrari.

BUELL XB9R FIREBOLT

Buell was formed in 1993 by a man called Erik Buell. He set up the firm with help from Harley-Davidson, the famous American motorcycle company. Harley-Davidson are not known for making fast bikes. But Buell had the idea of using a Harley **engine** in a lighter bike to make a really fast machine.

DID YOU KNOW?

Weighing just 175 kgs, the Firebolt is one of the lightest superbikes in the world.

The Firebolt has a belt instead of a chain to make the back wheel go round.

The Firebolt has **perimeter brakes** at the front. The brake disc is much bigger than normal, which means you can stop quicker.

STATS AND FACTS

LAUNCHED: *2002*

ORIGIN: *USA*

ENGINE: *984 cc*

CYLINDERS: *2*

MAX POWER: *92 bhp at 7,200 rpm*

MAX TORQUE: *92 NM at 5,500 rpm*

GEARS: *5*

DRY WEIGHT: *175 kg*

MAX SPEED: *130 mph (est)*

FUEL TANK CAPACITY: *14 litres*

COLOURS: *Arctic White, Battle Blue*

COST: *£7,345*

The Firebolt has several unusual features. The **exhaust** pipe, which is usually on the side of motorcycles, is underneath the Firebolt. The bike also has a hollow **frame**, which is used to store petrol.

HONDA CBR1100XX BLACKBIRD

The Japanese company Honda is one of the biggest motorcycle makers in the world. The Blackbird used to be the fastest motorcycle in the world, until Suzuki built the Hayabusa. With a few tweaks, the Blackbird can rocket to an incredible 200 mph.

DID YOU KNOW?

In 2001, a rider on a turbo-charged Blackbird did a wheelie at an amazing 200 mph!

The Blackbird has **linked brakes**. When you pull the front brake lever the back brake works too - and when you push the back brake pedal the front brake works as well.

The main Honda **sportsbike** is the CBR900RR Fireblade, which is smaller, lighter and faster than the Blackbird. It can go from 0 to 100 mph in 6 seconds.

STATS AND FACTS

LAUNCHED: *1996*

ORIGIN: *Japan*

ENGINE: *1,137 cc*

CYLINDERS: *4*

MAX POWER: *164 bhp at 9,200 rpm*

MAX TORQUE: *116 NM at 7,300 rpm*

GEARS: *6*

DRY WEIGHT: *223 kg*

MAX SPEED: *174 mph*

FUEL TANK CAPACITY: *24 litres*

COLOURS: *Black, Blue, Red*

COST: *£10,349*

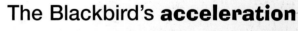

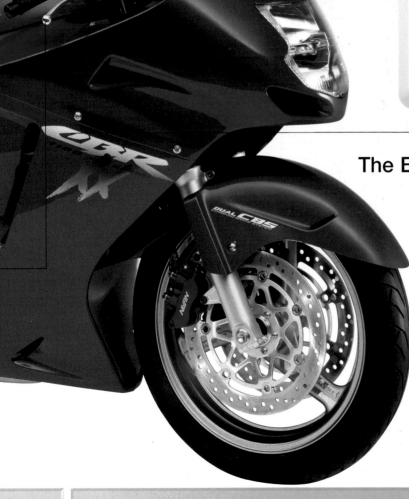

The Blackbird's **acceleration** is awesome. Thanks to its streamlined shape and huge **engine**, this bike can race from 0 to 130 mph in just 11 seconds.

KAWASAKI NINJA ZX-12R

The Japanese company Kawasaki have always made very fast motorcycles. The ZX-12R is the fastest bike on the planet, capable of just under 200 mph. The Ninja also has a big fuel **tank**, which means you can ride it long distances without stopping.

The ZX-12R has such good **brakes** that it is able to go from 70 mph to a stop in under 4 seconds.

The scoop under the **headlight** forces air into the **engine**, which drags extra fuel in. This gives the ZX-12R even more power.

DID YOU KNOW?

The ZX-12R has the widest back tyre of any sportsbike. It is a massive 200 mm wide!

STATS AND FACTS

LAUNCHED: *2000*

ORIGIN: *Japan*

ENGINE: *1,199 cc*

CYLINDERS: *4*

MAX POWER: *165 bhp at 9,800 rpm*

MAX TORQUE: *130 NM at 7,800*

GEARS: *6*

DRY WEIGHT: *210 kg*

MAX SPEED: *190 mph*

FUEL TANK CAPACITY: *20 litres*

COLOURS: *Black/Gold, Silver, Kawasaki Green*

COST: *£9,315*

The ZX-12R's **fairing** was made with help from Kawasaki's aircraft division. It was designed to make the bike as **aerodynamic** as possible.

HARLEY V-ROD

Famous for being the bikes that Hell's Angels like to ride, the Harley-Davidson has always been a bike for cruising on. There are lots of straight roads in America, and Harleys were made to ride long distances in comfort. However, the V-Rod is much sportier than other Harleys. It is the fastest bike the company have ever made.

DID YOU KNOW?

Despite being heavy motorcycles, the famous stunt rider Evel Knievel did all his jumps on a Harley-Davidson.

The V-Rod's fuel **tank** is under the seat. The space this saves leaves room for **air intakes**. These force more fuel into the bike's engine, supplying the V-Rod with extra power.

STATS AND FACTS

LAUNCHED: *2002*

ORIGIN: *USA*

ENGINE: *1,130 cc*

CYLINDERS: *2*

MAX POWER: *115 bhp at 8,000 rpm*

MAX TORQUE: *88 NM at 6,300 rpm*

GEARS: *5*

DRY WEIGHT: *270 kg*

MAX SPEED: *135 mph*

FUEL TANK CAPACITY: *15.1 litres*

COLOUR: *Anodised Aluminium*

COST: *£13,995*

There is a special badge on the V-Rod's tank. It says that the Harley-Davidson company have been making bikes for one hundred years.

The V-Rod has a brand new water-cooled **engine**. It was designed with the German sports car maker Porsche.

CAGIVA V-RAPTOR 1000

The Cagiva company built their first two motorcycles in 1978. A year later, they were building over 40,000 bikes a year. This mad-looking machine was designed for the company by the Italian Miguel Galluzzi.

DID YOU KNOW?

The name Cagiva is made up of 2 letters from the founder's surname and first name – Ca(stiglioni) Gi(ovanni) – and the first 2 letters of the company's hometown – Va(rese).

The Cagiva V-Raptor 1000 uses an **engine** made by the Japanese company Suzuki. The 'V' in the name describes the shape of the two **cylinders**.

This bike has claws! The V-Raptor has a strange set of talons by the passenger footrest.

STATS AND FACTS

LAUNCHED: *2000*

ORIGIN: *Italy*

ENGINE: *996 cc*

CYLINDERS: *2*

MAX POWER: *114 bhp at 8,500 rpm*

MAX TORQUE: *96 NM at 7,000 rpm*

GEARS: *6*

DRY WEIGHT: *197 kg*

MAX SPEED: *149 mph*

FUEL TANK CAPACITY: *18 litres*

COLOUR: *Red*

COST: *£7,149*

The bike is a 'Naked' sportbike. This means that there is no **bodywork**, or **fairing**, covering the engine.

DUCATI 999R

Ducati are an Italian motorbike company. The 999 is the fastest and most expensive Ducati. It comes in three versions – the 999, 999S and 999R. The 'R' is the fastest of the bikes, and is made of **carbon fibre** and **aluminium**.

This is a Ducati 749. It looks almost exactly the same as the 999R, but it has a 749 cc **engine**. This means it has less power and is a bit slower.

The 999R's seat and fuel **tank** can be moved backwards and forwards, and the footrests can be moved up and down. This Ducati can be made comfortable to ride, however tall or short you are.

STATS AND FACTS

LAUNCHED: *2002*

ORIGIN: *Italy*

ENGINE: *999 cc*

CYLINDERS: *2*

MAX POWER: *139 bhp at 10,000 rpm*

MAX TORQUE: *108 NM at 8,000 rpm*

GEARS: *6*

DRY WEIGHT: *193 kg*

MAX SPEED: *175 mph (est)*

FUEL TANK CAPACITY: *15.5 litres*

COLOURS: *Red or Yellow*

COST: *£19,300*

Each 999R has a unique silver badge to prove that it is a limited edition bike.

MV AGUSTA F4 SPR SENNA

MV Agusta is another Italian company with a racing history. Agusta bikes won 270 Grand Prix between 1950–1975 before the company ran out of money and closed. Then, in 1999, MV Agusta was brought back to life with the launch of the stunning F4. Lots of people think the Senna is the most beautiful bike in the world.

The Senna's **exhausts** come out under the seat, rather than at the side of the bike.

DID YOU KNOW?

Whenever a MV F4 Senna is sold, some of the money is given to educate Brazilian children.

STATS AND FACTS

LAUNCHED: *2002*

ORIGIN: *Italy*

ENGINE: *749 cc*

CYLINDERS: *4*

MAX POWER: *140 bhp at 12,600 rpm*

MAX TORQUE: *81 NM at 10,500 rpm*

GEARS: *6*

DRY WEIGHT: *188 kg*

MAX SPEED: *177 mph*

FUEL TANK CAPACITY: *20 litres*

COLOURS: *Grey and Red*

COST: *£17,350*

The Senna's twin **headlights** are arranged on top of each other. This makes the front of the bike more **aerodynamic**.

The Senna was made in memory of the famous Formula 1 racing driver Ayrton Senna. Only 300 were made.

SUZUKI GSX 1300R HAYABUSA

The Japanese bike maker Suzuki was formed in 1952. In 1998 they built a new motorcycle called the Hayabusa. At the time, the Hayabusa was the fastest bike in the world. This monster's **engine** is actually bigger than those found in many cars.

DID YOU KNOW?

A Hayabusa is so powerful that it can wear out a back tyre in as little as a thousand miles.

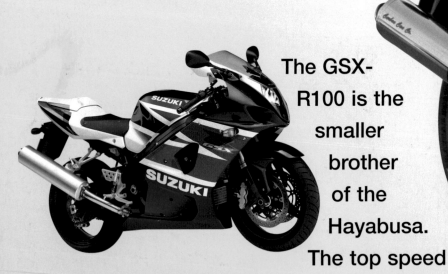

The GSX-R100 is the smaller brother of the Hayabusa. The top speed is the same as the Hayabusa, but this bike has better **acceleration** because it is lighter.

The British Land Speed Record for a motorcycle is held by a **turbo-charged** Hayabusa. This bike reached a speed in excess of 241 mph!

STATS AND FACTS

LAUNCHED: *1998*

ORIGIN: *Japan*

ENGINE: *1,298 cc*

CYLINDERS: *4*

MAX POWER: *155 bhp at 9,000 rpm*

MAX TORQUE: *134 NM at 6,800 rpm*

GEARS: *6*

DRY WEIGHT: *215 kg*

MAX SPEED: *186 mph*

FUEL TANK CAPACITY: *18 litres*

COLOURS: *Blue & Black, Blue & Silver, Silver*

COST: *£8,299*

The Hayabusa is a Japanese bird of prey that eats blackbirds. Suzuki called their new **superbike** a Hayabusa because it is faster and more powerful than Honda's CBR1100XX Blackbird, its main rival.

YAMAHA YZF R1

The Yamaha Motor Company is one of the best known motorcycle producers in the world. Originally a maker of musical instruments, the firm started to make motorcycles after the Second World War. In 2002 Yamaha launched the latest version of their incredibly successful R1 bike, which has competed in the British Superbike Championship.

DID YOU KNOW?

The Yamaha R1 will do over 75 mph in first gear, and over 100 mph in second gear.

The R1 has no light bulbs at the back. Instead it is fitted with tiny **LEDs** (Light Emitting Diodes). If one stops working, there are still another 20 providing light.

STATS AND FACTS

LAUNCHED: *1998*

ORIGIN: *Japan*

ENGINE: *998 cc*

CYLINDERS: *4*

MAX POWER: *152 bhp at 10,500 rpm*

MAX TORQUE: *107 NM at 8,500 rpm*

GEARS: *6*

DRY WEIGHT: *174 kg*

MAX SPEED: *176 mph*

FUEL TANK CAPACITY: *18 litres*

COLOURS: *Blue, Red, White*

COST: *£9,134*

One of Yamaha's most popular bikes is the YZF-R6. It isn't as fast as an R1. But because it is small and light it can keep up with most bigger bikes on twisty racetracks and roads.

To make the new R1 even quicker, Yamaha have given it a lighter **chassis** and wheels. The front and back of the bike are also more pointed and **aerodynamic**.

CALIFORNIA QUAKE DRAG BOAT

The fastest racing boats on the water are drag boats. These single seater craft surge like rockets at breathtaking speeds over the waves, often spending more time above the surface than on it. This incredible machine has reached speeds of about 230 mph!

DID YOU KNOW?

Drag boat racing attracts crowds of up to one million people.

The Californian Quake's 5,000 **hp** engine let it become the first boat to race to ¼ mile in under 5 seconds - a world record!

Bottled air is supplied to the driver's helmet. This is so in the event of a crash, he can carry on breathing whilst waiting for divers to rescue him.

STATS AND FACTS

LAUNCHED: *1999*

ORIGIN: *USA*

ENGINES: *500 cubic inch nitromethane engine generating 5,000 hp*

LENGTH: *7.62 metres*

WIDTH: *3.72 metres*

MAX SPEED: *198 knots (230 mph)*

MAX WEIGHT: *4.75 tonnes*

LOAD: *1 pilot*

FUEL CAPACITY: *20 litres*

COST: *£60,000*

The most important part of the boat is the safety capsule. Complete with **rollcage**, it breaks free from the boat in the event of a high speed crash.

JUNE LEE CHINESE JUNK

The junk is one of the oldest boat designs. The first types were sailing over 2,000 years ago. Later they were used for trading goods all around East Asia. Junks still carry goods today - from rice and timber to computers and cars!

The **sails** are made of woven **linen** or similar fibres. They are held together by a frame made from long poles of bamboo or wood.

DID YOU KNOW?

Today the word 'junk' means old rubbish. But long ago it was an important word in Chinese – 'chu-ong', meaning 'boat'.

STATS AND FACTS

The **hull** is divided into separate compartments by cross-walls called **bulkheads**. If water leaks into one, it cannot spread to the others, so the ship stays afloat.

LAUNCHED: *1962*

ORIGIN: *Thailand*

ENGINES: *One generating 380 hp*

LENGTH: *33 metres*

WIDTH: *8.5 metres*

MAX SPEED: *8 knots (9.2 mph)*

MAX WEIGHT: *5.4 tonnes*

LOAD: *10 person crew plus 18 passengers*

FUEL CAPACITY: *10,000 litres*

COST: *£1.25 million*

Many junks now have **engines**, for when the wind drops. They also have **satellite navigation** to help them find their way.

ILLBRUCK RACING YACHT

Every year the fastest yachts in the world get together for the *Round The World Yacht Race*. In 2002 it was won by illbrook. The eight yachts in the competition covered over 37,000 miles in total, taking almost nine months.

DID YOU KNOW?

The whole illbrook project - yacht, crew, back-up team, equipment, training, transport, supplies - cost nearly £16 million.

Round-the-world yachts battle giant waves, howling gales, collisions with icebergs and whales - and each other!

STATS AND FACTS

LAUNCHED: *2002*

ORIGIN: *Germany*

ENGINES: *n/a*

LENGTH: *19.5 metres*

WIDTH: *5.25 metres*

MAX SPEED: *36.75 knots (42 mph)*

MAX WEIGHT: *13.5 tonnes*

LOAD: *12 people*

COST: *£16 million*

Crews pull the cables for the **sails** using high-speed **winches** with long handles. The height of the tallest mast is 26 metres.

The illbruck's **satellite** communications centre contains telephone, email and video transmission facilities.

JAMES CLARK ROSS RESEARCH SHIP

One of the world's toughest ships, the James Clark Ross can smash its way through ice more than two metres thick. This vessel is actually a huge floating **laboratory**, used for exploring and carrying out scientific research in the freezing seas of Antarctica.

There are five main sets of laboratories and science rooms on board the James Clark Ross. More can be loaded onto the **deck**, in house-sized containers.

JAMES CLARK ROSS

The main **hull** is extra-strong. It is made of very thick **steel**, capable of pushing through ice and fending off bergs.

STATS AND FACTS

LAUNCHED: *1990*

ORIGIN: *Britain*

ENGINES: *Two x Wartsilla R32 (3.1 MW each) and two x Warsilla R22 (1.0 MW) engines delivering 8,500 hp*

LENGTH: *99 metres*

WIDTH: *18.85 metres*

MAX SPEED: *15.7 knots (18 mph)*

MAX WEIGHT: *5,732 tonnes*

LOAD: *12 officers, 15 crew, 1 doctor, 31 scientists (maximum)*

FUEL CAPACITY: *1,350 cubic metres*

COST: *£37.5 million*

DID YOU KNOW?

A compressed air system prevents ice from squeezing and cracking the hull by rolling the ship from side-to-side.

James Clark Ross surveys the oceans, and measures depths and currents. It also acts as a floating weather station, and even searches for strange creatures of the deep.

LOS ANGELES FIREBOAT NO. 2

Although ships are surrounded by water, they sometimes catch fire. Their **engines** and fuel may go up in flames, or they might carry a cargo like oil, which can burn. Almost every big port has fireboats on hand to tackle emergencies. This vessel is one of the Los Angeles Fire Department's six fireboats.

DID YOU KNOW?

Firefighters wear breathing kits. This is because some kinds of poisonous smoke can kill in just a few seconds.

All parts of the fireboat are flameproof, in case there is an explosion of burning fuel nearby.

2 LOS ANGELES CITY FIRE

STATS AND FACTS

LAUNCHED: *1925*

ORIGIN: *USA*

ENGINES: *Two 700 hp V-12 Cummins; three 380 hp 6 cylinder in-line Cummins; and two 525 hp V-12 2 cycle Detroits, plus six engines for pumps*

LENGTH: *30 metres*

WIDTH: *6 metres*

MAX SPEED: *17 knots (19.6 mph)*

MAX WEIGHT: *152 tonnes*

LOAD: *14 crew*

FUEL CAPACITY: *9,801 litres*

COST: *£135,550 (in 1925)*

When dockside buildings catch fire, it is time to call in the fireboats. As well as fighting ordinary fires, they can tackle electrical blazes by spraying special foam rather than water.

Six powerful diesel-powered **pumps**, all with their own engines, suck in water from around the boat. Then they fire out powerful **jets** of water from water-guns. These can reach heights of more than 150 metres.

NIMITZ-CLASS AIRCRAFT CARRIER

Nimitz-class aircraft carriers are the biggest warships ever built. Each of these US giants is a floating army, navy and air force. The Nimitz-class has a crew the size of a small town, which includes 3,360 ships crew and 2,500 air crew. This number doesn't even include the soldiers and pilots!

This supercarrier carries up to 85 planes and six helicopters, along with all their spares, tools, pilots and service crew. Jet fuel is stored in swimming-pool-sized tanks.

STATS AND FACTS

LAUNCHED: *1972*

ORIGIN: *USA*

ENGINES: *Two nuclear reactors powering 4 steam turbines producing 260,000 hp*

LENGTH: *333 metres*

WIDTH: *40.8 metres*

MAX SPEED: *More than 30 knots (35 mph)*

MAX WEIGHT: *Over 100,000 tonnes*

LOAD: *3,360 ships crew and 2,500 air crew*

COST: *£1.25 billion*

Supercarriers like the Nimitz-class aircraft carrier are equipped with the latest computers, **radar**, missiles and other equipment. It takes three years to re-fuel, re-equip and re-fit these monsters.

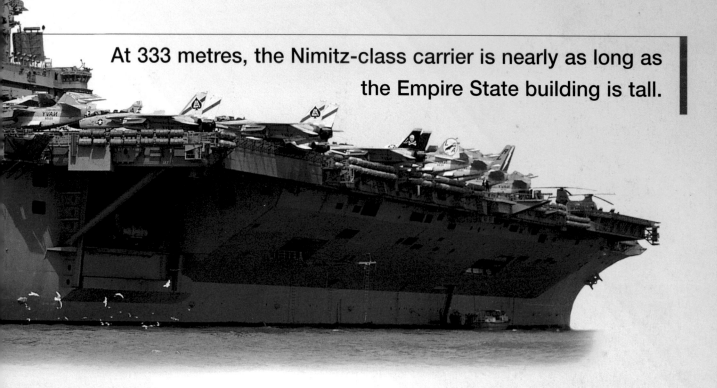

At 333 metres, the Nimitz-class carrier is nearly as long as the Empire State building is tall.

JAHRE VIKING OIL SUPERTANKER

The biggest ships in the world are the giant tankers which carry crude oil, or petroleum. Their precious cargo is used to make petrol and other fuels, but also plastics, paints and hundreds of other products. These huge tankers are bigger than islands and take 5 miles to slow down and stop!

DID YOU KNOW?

The holds in the Jahre Viking could hold St Paul's cathedral in London four times over.

Most of the ship is controlled by computer. The crew is usually about 35-40. They control the vessel and live in the comparatively small **stern** section of the ship.

Oil is pumped on board through pipes at the oil terminal or rig. It is pumped off again at a **refinery**.

STATS AND FACTS

LAUNCHED: *1979*

ORIGIN: *Japan*

ENGINES: *Four steam turbines (37,300 KW) generating 50,019 hp each*

LENGTH: *940 metres*

WIDTH: *141 metres*

MAX SPEED: *10 knots (11.5 mph)*

MAX WEIGHT: *647,955 tonnes fully laden, 564,763 tonnes, unladen*

CREW: *35 to 40 people*

LOAD: *4,240,865 barrels of oil*

FUEL CAPACITY: *20,000 litres*

COST: *£62.5 million*

The whole **deck** area can be as large as four soccer pitches. It can take several minutes to walk the length of the deck, so crew members sometimes use bicycles to get around!

POLARIS VIRAGE TX JETSKI

The jetski is a combination of motorcycle, water-ski and snow-mobile. These vehicles are used for surging across the waves at great speeds. You can also do stunts on them, and even turn somersaults! If you lose your grip and fall off the craft, the water-jet stops immediately.

DID YOU KNOW?

The jetski was developed in the late 1960s. The idea came from US motorcycle rider Clay Jacobson who was working for the Kawasaki Motorcycle Company at the time.

The engine turns a fan-like **impeller**. This sucks in water in through a large opening, and blasts it out the back as a fast, narrow **jet**.

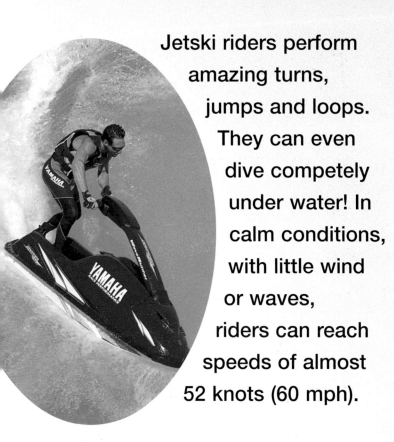

Jetski riders perform amazing turns, jumps and loops. They can even dive competely under water! In calm conditions, with little wind or waves, riders can reach speeds of almost 52 knots (60 mph).

STATS AND FACTS

LAUNCHED: *2000*

ORIGIN: *USA*

ENGINE: *Polaris Marine 1200, producing 135 hp*

LENGTH: *3.06 metres*

WIDTH: *1.25 metres*

MAX SPEED: *52 knots (60 mph)*

MAX WEIGHT: *285 kg*

LOAD: *1 pilot*

FUEL CAPACITY: *77 litres*

COST: *Up to £8,000*

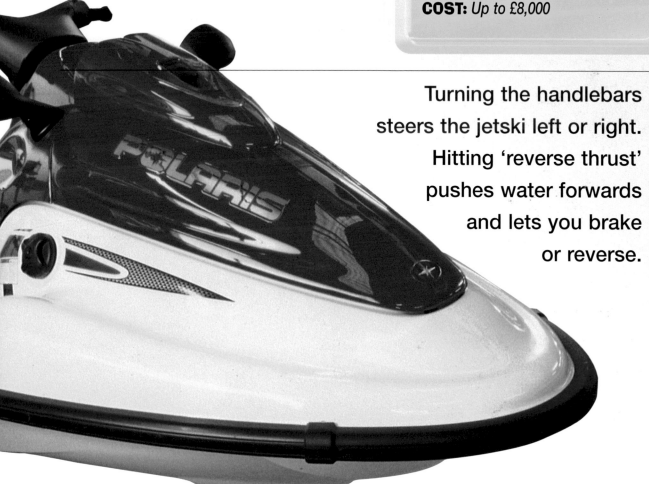

Turning the handlebars steers the jetski left or right. Hitting 'reverse thrust' pushes water forwards and lets you brake or reverse.

THE WORLD LUXURY LINER

The World is a luxury **liner** with a difference - you live on it! For a vast price you can buy a set of rooms on board to make your permanent home. The ship travels to exciting world events, including the Rio de Janeiro carnival in Brazil and the Formula 1 Motor Race in Monaco.

DID YOU KNOW?

The cost of an apartment on The World ranges from £1.25 million to over £6 million.

The 12 **decks** have every luxury you can imagine. There are seven restaurants, a casino, a nightclub, theatres, gyms, tennis courts, swimming pools and cinemas.

STATS AND FACTS

LAUNCHED: *2001*

ORIGIN: *Norway*

ENGINES: *Two Wartsila 12 cylinder diesels, generating 5520 kW (7402 hp)*

LENGTH: *196.35 metres*

WIDTH: *29.8 metres*

MAX SPEED: *18.5 knots (21 mph)*

MAX WEIGHT: *43,524 tonnes*

LOAD: *Maximum of 976 residents, guests and crew*

FUEL CAPACITY: *1,150 cubic metres*

COST: *£164 million*

On The World, people are not passengers, but residents on a lifetime's holiday. There are 110 main residences, plus 88 extra apartments which can be rented out to guests.

The **hull** of The World was built using giant pieces of **steel**, lifted into place using giant cranes.

TRENT-TYPE LIFEBOAT

Every sailor has two terrible fears - shipwreck and drowning at sea. Brave lifeboat crews are always ready for rescue missions, and their boats must stay safe, even in the worst storms. The powerful Trent-type lifeboats are run by Britain's RNLI (Royal National Lifeboat Institution).

The hull of this lifeboat is made of various plastics, **carbon fibres** and other **composites**. Unlike metal these are very light but also very strong, and they never rust.

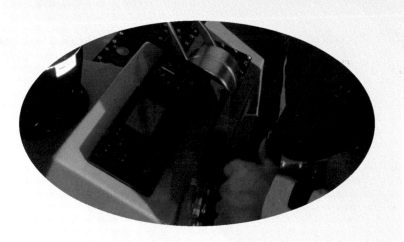

Special **radar** and radio equipment can track ships in distress. This technology uses the Marsat and Sarsat emergency **satellite navigation** systems.

STATS AND FACTS

LAUNCHED: *1994*

ORIGIN: *Britain*

ENGINES: *Two MAN diesels, 808 hp per engine, each about as powerful as a Formula 1 racing car engine*

LENGTH: *14.26 metres*

MAX SPEED: *25 knots (29 mph)*

MAX WEIGHT: *27.5 tonnes)*

LOAD: *6 crew plus 10 survivors*

FUEL CAPACITY: *4,100 litres*

COST: *£1.25 million*

The survivor's **cabin** has seats for 10 people. There are also heaters, dry clothes and a small **galley** serving hot drinks and snacks.

GLOSSARY

Acceleration Making a vehicle go faster.

Aerodynamic A shape that cuts through the air around it.

Air intakes Large scoops that direct air into the engine, sucking in extra fuel to give a bike more power.

Air refuelling Method of refuelling military aircraft whilst in flight, via a fuel hose linked to a tanker aircraft.

Aluminium A lightweight, but strong, metal.

Afterburner System which injects extra fuel into the exhaust gases of a plane to provide large amounts of extra power.

Bark Another name for a ship.

BHP Brake horse power, the usual measure of an engine's power.

Body Outer part of a car that covers the chassis and engine.

Bodywork Plastic panels which cover the chassis and engine.

Boosters Large canisters containing fuel that are attached to the sides of a space rocket as it is launched.

Brakes Part of a vehicle used to slow it down.

Bridge A ship's main control room from where it is steered. It is usually situated high up to provide good views in all directions.

Bulkheads Dividing 'walls' that run across the inside of a ship, from side to side. They have doors for people to pass through.

Buoyancy The upwards pushing force that water gives to objects, causing them to float if they are light enough.

Cabin An enclosed area on a ship, aircraft or spacecraft that holds the crew, passengers and cargo.

Carbon fibre A modern lightweight material used to make lots of types of vehicles.

Catamaran A boat or ship with two hulls, joined together by a wide deck or decks over the top.

CC Cubic capacity, the measurement used for the size of the engine.

Chassis The part which holds the engine, wheels and body together.

Cockpit The part of an aircraft where the pilot and his assistants sit.

Composite A material or substance which is made of a mixture of materials, such as plastics, metals and fibre-glass. Composites are usually very light and very strong.

Convertible (See Roadster).

Coupé A two-door hard top car.

Cylinder The part of the engine where fuel is burned to make energy.

Dashboard The panel behind the steering wheel that usually contains the speedometer and other dials.

Decks The main floors or storeys of a ship, and especially the uppermost flat area where people walk about.

Dynamic stability control A driver aid which can safely brake any or all four wheels.

Ejection seat A seat, usually fitted in military aircraft, that can be fired or ejected from the aircraft.

Engine The part of a vehicle where fuel is burned to create energy.

Exhaust Pipe at the back of the vehicle where poisonous gases made when fuel is burned are let out. In cars and bikes, the exhaust is also used to reduce engine noise.

Fairing The front and side parts of the bodywork.

Fans Part of the bike that pushes or pulls cool air through the radiator, helping to cool the engine.

Foreplanes Moveable surfaces at the front of a plane that provide extra lift and balance.

Forks The fork-shaped tubes that hold the front wheel and handlebars in place.

Formula One Famous motor racing championship.

Four-wheel drive A car that has power delivered to all four wheels.

Frame The part of the bike which holds the engine, wheels and bodywork together. Sometimes called the chassis.

Freighter An aircraft made to carry cargo rather than passengers.

Fuselage See Cabin.

Galley The kitchen or dining area on a ship.

Gearchange paddles Levers on a steering wheel used to change up and down gears.

Gears System that lets a car or bike go faster or slower without damaging the engine.

Headlight The bright light at the front of the car or bike.

Hold The lower part of a plane where cargo is stored.

Horsepower (HP) The measure of an engine's power, originally based on the power of an engine compared to a horse.

Hull The main part or body of a ship, which floats on the water.

Impeller A fan-shaped propeller or screw in a tube, that sucks water through the tube.

Jet Stream of fluid forced out under pressure from a narrow opening or nozzle.

Jets Part of an engine that provides the lifting power for an aircraft.

Jib A triangular sail usually at the front of a yacht or sailing ship.

Jumbo Another name for a Boeing 747.

Knot One nautical mile per hour, equal to 1.15 miles per hour or 1.85 kilometres per hour.

Laser guided bomb A bomb launched from an aircraft that has sensors in its nose to guide it onto a target.

LED Light Emitting Diode, a source of light used in some brake lights.

Linen Hardwearing material often used to make a ship's sails.

Liner A large ship that carries passengers.

Linked brakes System where the front brake lever also works the back brake, and the back brake lever works the front brake.

Mach Measurement which relates the speed of an aircraft to the speed of sound. Mach 1 is the speed of sound (700 mph) Mach 2 is twice the speed of sound.

Mast A tall pole on a ship which may hold up sails, radio aerials, radar dishes or even flags

Nose The front end of a car or an aircraft.

Orbiter A spacecraft or satellite designed to orbit a planet or other body without landing on it.

Parachute A large canopy with a body harness underneath. It is designed to slow the rate of descent of a person from an aircraft.

Perimeter brakes Braking system where the brake disc is mounted round the edge of the wheel.

Pilot A person qualified to fly an aircraft or spaceship.

Propeller A machine with spinning blades that provides thrust to lift an aircraft.

Pump A machine used for raising water or other liquids.

Radar A system using invisible radio waves, beamed out and reflected back by objects as 'echoes'. These are displayed on a screen to help identify other ships, planes, land, icebergs and similar items.

Radial Brakes Braking system where the brake discs are mounted at the bottom of the forks, parallel to the wheel.

Radiator A device through which water or other fluids flow to keep the engine cool.

Refinery Place where oil is turned into petrol.

Rigged A ship fitted with sails, and the ropes and chains used to control them.

Roadster A car with a roof that can be folded back or removed.

Rollcage A metal framework within some vehicles that prevents crushing in the event of it turning over in a crash.

RPM Revolutions (revs) of the engine per minute.

Rudder A large, wide, flat part which can be tilted from side to side for steering. Usually situated at the rear or stern of a ship.

Sails Fabric spread to catch or deflect the wind as a means of propelling a ship or boat.

Satellite navigation A system which tells you where you are, using satellites in space.

Scramjet A hydrogen-fuelled engine designed for flying at five times the speed of sound.

Sensors Devices that help pilots fly their aircraft, detect enemy aircraft, or fire weapons accurately.

Spoiler A lightweight panel attached to a car to prevent the vehicle lifting up at high speeds.

Sportsbike A fast motorcycle that has been developed for road use.

Stealth technology Technology used to make a plane almost invisible.

Steel Very strong metal.

Stern The rear part of a ship or boat.

Submersible A boat that can function when under water.

Superbike A fast motorcycle that is very similar to a race bike.

Supersonic Faster than the speed of sound.

Suspension Springs and shock absorbers attached to the wheels of a car or bike, giving a smooth ride even on bumpy surfaces.

Tail The rear of the car, or the rear part of the fuselage that balances a plane.

Tank Hollow metal unit where petrol is stored.

Targa A hard top car with a removable roof panel.

Throttle The part of a bike that is used to make it go faster or slower.

Thrust A pushing force created in a jet engine or rocket that gives aircraft enough speed to take off.

Titanium alloy A light, strong and heat-tolerant material.

Topgallant The top part of a ship's mast.

Torque The force with which engine power can be delivered to a car's wheels.

Traction control A driver aid that helps tyres grip the road.

Turbine Machine with a wheel or rotor driven by water, steam or gases.

Turbo System that increases a vehicle's power by forcing more air into the engine.

Tyre A rubber covering for a wheel, filled with compressed air.

V/Inline/flat The arrangement of the cylinders in the engine.

V8/V12 The engine size given in number of cylinders.

Valve Device that controls the flow of petrol into the engine.

VIFF Vectoring in Forward Flight. System that lets a plane change direction very suddenly.

VTOL Vertical Take-Off, Vertical Landing. System that holds an aircraft in the air as it takes off or lands.

Winches System that lifts something by winding a line around a reel.

Wings Part of the aircraft that provides lift, placed on either side of the fuselage.

Wingspan The distance between the tips of the wings of an aircraft.

INDEX

INDEX

The ultimate guide to amazing
MACHINES

By David Kimber, Bill Gunston, Jeff Painter, Richard Newland and Steve Parker

Stats and Facts • Top makes
Top models • Top speeds

Copyright © ticktock Entertainment Ltd 2006
First published in Great Britain in 2006 by ticktock Media Ltd.,
Unit 2, Orchard Business Centre, North Farm Road, Tunbridge Wells, Kent, TN2 3XF
ISBN 1-86007-966-0
Printed in Hong Kong

Picture credits
Cars: All images Car Photo Library-www.carphoto.co.uk
Planes: Corbis: 28-29, 46-47. Aviation Picture Library: 30-31, 32-33, 36-37, 38-39, 40-41. Lockheed: 42-43.
NASA: 34-35, 44-45, 48-49.
Motorbikes: All images Car Photo Library-www.carphoto.co.uk
Boats: Alamy: 74-75, 85. Beken of Cowes: 76c, 82-83c. British Antarctic Survey: 78-79. Corbis: 80-81, 83t, 84c.
John Clark Photography: 72-73c. RNLI: 90-91. World of Residensea: 88-89. Yamaha: 87t.

The publishers would like to thank Keith Faulkner of Jane's Defence Weekly, Richard Newland of Fast Bikes
magazine, Jamie Asher, Sam Petter and Tim Bones.

BOMBER BOYS